KNOWLEDGE ENCYCLOPEDIA
MARINE ANIMALS

Wonder House

(An imprint of Prakash Books)

contact@wonderhousebooks.com

Disclaimer: The information contained in this encyclopedia has been collated with inputs from subject experts. All information contained herein is true to the best of the Publisher's knowledge. Maps are only indicative in nature.

ISBN : 9789354400162

Table of Contents

HOW IT ALL BEGAN

The first fish evolved about 510 million years ago. The evolution of these organisms marks the beginning of complex life which would ultimately result in the evolution of human beings. Fish and marine animals evolved along the same time, dominating the waters of Earth.

The first fish took birth in the oceans and belonged to a class of animals called vertebrates (animals that have backbones). Besides fish, the waters are home to marine animals such as octopuses and sponges. It is important to remember that many marine animals are invertebrates, which means they do not have backbones. Read on to find out some incredible facts about these beings that live under water.

▼ Fish and other marine animals often compete with each other for food

The Evolution of Fish

Rewind to 540 million years ago, to a time called the Cambrian Period. Unlike today, the vegetation then was not so evolved or diverse. In fact, the land was inhospitable for life. However, the oceans were bursting with life and this period was called the 'Cambrian Explosion'. The fossil for the first known vertebrate evolved during this period and was called *Haikouichthys ercaicunensis*. The fossil for the earliest primitive **chordate**, called *Pikaia gracilens*, also dates to this period.

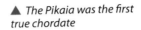

🐾 Like an Eel

Pikaia gracilens resembled the modern eels. The animal was small, with a tapered, streamlined body. It had eyes, a brain, and a **notochord**. This refers to a flexible, rod-like structure found in the embryos of all vertebrates. It goes on to become a part of the backbone.

▲ *The Pikaia was the first true chordate*

🐾 Jawless Wonder

You might not recognise the first fish to swim on Earth as they had no jaws or teeth. They began to appear in the Ordovician Period, about 488 million years ago. During this period, Earth looked very different from how it looks today. The ocean covered the area to the north of the tropics and land was limited to a supercontinent called **Gondwana**.

The (now extinct) jawless fish of this period were called ostracoderms. Not more than 30 cm in length, they lived in fresh water and had bony scales which protected the brain. They were bottom feeders, which means they found food on the ocean floor.

▲ *The extinct lampreys were jawless fish*

🐾 The Jaws Emerged

The *Acanthodians* (or spiny shark) were among the first fish with jaws. They emerged in the Silurian Period, about 440 million years ago. During this period, there were large-scale geographical changes due to the melting of giant glaciers. This resulted in a rise in sea levels.

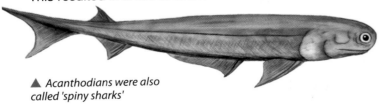

▲ *Acanthodians were also called 'spiny sharks'*

The fish that existed during the Silurian Period survived for about 150–180 million years before they went extinct. Nothing is known about their ancestors, but it is assumed that they originated from the jawless invertebrates.

The *Acanthodians* were small fish with huge eyes and short snouts, indicating that they relied more upon their vision rather than smell. They had bony spines in front of the fins and small, diamond-shaped scales. They had about four fins that they used for manoeuvring rather than locomotion. The latter was managed with the tail.

👤 In Real Life

Sharks are not bony, but **cartilaginous**. Hence, unlike reptiles, mammals, and birds, the skeletons of sharks are made of cartilage and tissue. Human beings also have cartilage in their ears and nose. You might be able to feel it by placing a finger on the tip of your nose. Cartilage has lesser density than bone, and it is more flexible.

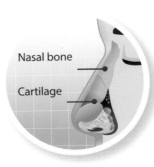

Nasal bone

Cartilage

The Age of the Fish

The period from 420–358 million years ago is called the Devonian Period. It came to be called the 'Age of Fish' because of the variety and wealth of fish that swam in the waters of this period. Among the many species of fish, the placoderms dominated the waters for almost 70 million years, disappearing at the end of the Devonian Period.

The word 'placoderm' means 'plate skin' and as the name suggests, the fish were covered with bony armour, especially around the head and the trunk. The tail was well-developed. The other important features of this fish type were the presence of jaws, with attached tooth-like structures; and the development of well-formed fins at the pectoral and maybe even the pelvic region.

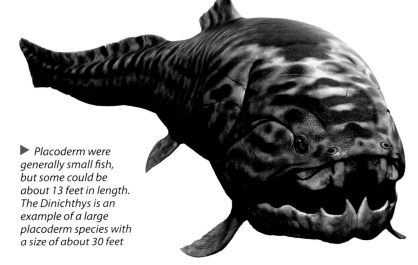

▶ Placoderm were generally small fish, but some could be about 13 feet in length. The Dinichthys is an example of a large placoderm species with a size of about 30 feet

Ancestors of Modern Fish

The earliest shark-like fish appeared in the Devonian Period. They were the first cartilaginous fish to appear, belonging to the group called *Chondrichthyes*. While most of these primitive fish disappeared, few still survived and evolved.

The modern sharks, skates, and ray-fish are cartilaginous fish that originated in the Jurassic Period, about 200 million years ago. During this period, the dry, hot climate changed to subtropical and humid.

The cartilaginous fish had flexible jaws. They could battle with fish that were bigger than themselves. A tail fin helped them swim faster and longer so they could easily pursue their prey.

Isn't It Amazing!

Megalodon, meaning 'big tooth', was a huge 25,000-kilogram shark that grew almost 55 feet in length. It had a gaping mouth of 6 feet. Megalodon had sharp teeth which could eat anything, big or small, in the ocean. Each tooth was about 17.7 centimetres in length.

This shark appeared 16 million years ago. It ruled the ocean until two million years ago, when it disappeared. It is now extinct because of extensive changes in the ocean temperatures and lack of prey. But folklore says it still lurks deep in the oceans!

▼ The megalodon is said to be the largest fish that ever swam the waters of our planet

▼ The prehistoric Stethacanthus shark had a strange anvil-shaped dorsal fin on its back. No one knows what it was used for

▶ Helicoprion was another ancient shark. It had a spiral-shaped tooth structure called the tooth-whorl

Whorls ●

Anatomy of a Fish

With over 35,000 fish species in the world, scientists have identified important body parts of the animal. These can help distinguish between the various species that swim in the waters of our planet.

 Body

Fish have streamlined bodies which help them move smoothly in water. The shape of the body and the tail have evolved in accordance with their habitat. The shape of the body decides a fish's ability to swim. For example, tuna fish are excellent swimmers and have sharp, forked tails that make them agile.

▲ *Most fish have taste buds all over their body*

Scales

Lateral line

▶ *Fish survive in water with the aid of these parts*

Caudal fin

Anal fin

 Fins

Fish use their fins to swim. The position of the fins on the body determines their functionality. Fish move forward with their tail fins, whereas they use the pectoral fins to swim and balance better. The dorsal fins are used for protection and balance. The ventral and anal fins located on the belly are needed for balance and steering.

 Mouth

If a fish has a superior (upward pointing) mouth, it will eat food above it. If a fish has an inferior (downward pointing) mouth, it will eat food from the bottom of the seabed.

 Gills

Instead of lungs, fish take in oxygen molecules dissolved in the water through their gills. These are located on both sides of their mouths. They are covered by a series of bones called the operculum. Some fish species have spikes on their gills to protect themselves against predators. Water passes over the tiny network of blood vessels in the gills. The fish force the water to move over the gills using their mouth and throat.

▲ *A close-up of the gills of a fish*

Scales

Most fish have an external covering of scales which act like a protective device. They are unique to fish. Scales come in different sizes and colours; they vary among species and at times even sexes. Like human skin, they protect the fish. The scales are covered by a slimy, mucous layer that protects the fish from bacteria in the water.

Dorsal fins

Lateral Line

Lateral lines are located under the scales of a fish and consist of many tiny openings or holes. These lines run parallel to the fish's body and allow it to feel low vibrations in the water.

Nares

Nares are located on the snouts. They are the two holes that help a fish smell under water. Some fish have a heightened sense of smell because of the nares.

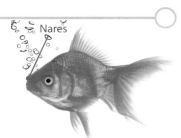

Nares

▲ The goldfish have nares which allow them to smell better than human beings

Eye

Nares or nostrils

Mouth

Gill

Gill cover

Pectoral fin

Pelvic fin

Gas Chamber

Most fish do not breathe with their lungs. Instead they have a swim bladder, also called the air bladder. This is a gas-filled sac in their abdominal region. It contains a mixture of oxygen, carbon dioxide, and nitrogen absorbed from the blood. It functions as a **ballast** organ, which means it helps the fish maintain depth without sinking or floating upward. The swim bladder amplifies sound in some fish, like the glass fish. This part is missing in cartilaginous fish, deep-sea dwelling fish, and in a few bony fish.

▲ One can clearly see the swim bladder of a glassfish as it is transparent

Heart

Fish's internal organs such as the stomach, gall bladder, liver, and kidney are similar to mammals. But their hearts are different. While human hearts have four chambers, fish hearts have only two—one chamber receives blood and the other chamber pumps it out.

Conus arteriosus

Ventricle

Atrium

Sinus arteriosus

 ▶ If a fish's blood pressure is too high, it might damage the gills of the fish

Fishy Features

The word 'fish' comes from the Old English word 'fisc'. It was used for any animal living in water. To us human beings, from where we stand at the highest position on the evolutionary scale, fish might seem like just another set of animals that cohabit Earth with us. But these forms, which are at the base of the evolutionary scale, have many interesting tales to tell.

Cold-blooded

Fish are **ectotherms** or cold-blooded animals. No, their blood is not cold, as the name suggests. It just means that they cannot regulate their body temperatures internally and rely on external sources such as sunlight or shade to maintain it. Most often, their temperatures tend to be slightly lower than that of the environment to prevent loss of moisture.

Cold-blooded animals use interesting adaptations to overcome the inability to regulate their body temperature. Some species of frogs become **dormant** in the warm weather to prevent moisture loss. Ocean fish stay hydrated by drinking lots of water.

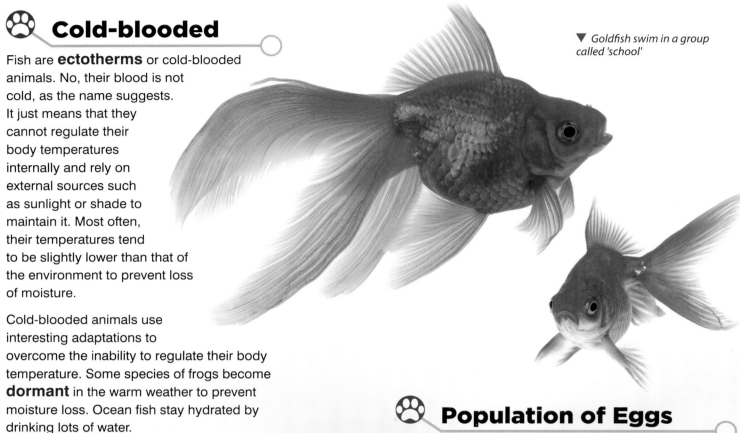

▼ *Goldfish swim in a group called 'school'*

Vertebrates

It is with the fish that the world got its first vertebrates. A vertebrae or backbone supports the body and protects the spinal cord. So, vertebrates need their backbones and brains to survive.

Population of Eggs

Fish lay several eggs at one time. This ensures that the reproduction process is successful. In fish, fertilisation takes place outside the body. In most cases, the fertilised eggs are not looked after by the adults. This exposes the eggs to predators and other dangers that could reduce the number of eggs drastically. So, not all eggs lead to successful reproduction. Those that fail to hatch are recycled into the ecosystem.

Laying Eggs

Fish lay their eggs in water. However, unlike mammals, birds, and reptiles, they do not lay amniotic eggs, that is, eggs containing **amnion**. Amnion is a fluid-filled sac that keeps the embryos moist.

◀ *A siamese female fighting fish guarding her newly laid eggs amongst the bubble nest*

Isn't It Amazing!

A unique feature of the clownfish is that they are all born male during birth. If their group is missing a dominant female, one clownfish will change its sex. They cannot change back to male. This is because a school of clownfish follows a hierarchy. The most dominant female rules the school. So, if there is no dominant female, the dominant male changes sex. Similarly, moray eels and gobies also change sex.

A History of Jawless Fish

There are so many fish on this planet. Even within the same species, there is a great diversity. For example, though the hammerhead shark and tiger shark belong to the same species, they look quite different. So, in order to study fish, scientists have classified them into three broad groups according to their features. These groups are the jawless fish, cartilaginous fish, and bony fish.

Primitive Jawless Fish

Agnathans comprise the early species of jawless fish. This includes lampreys, hagfish and other extinct groups of fish. The core identifiers of these fish are the absence of jaws, paired fins, pelvic fins, and vertebral columns. They have slimy skin and a cartilaginous skeleton, instead of a bony skeleton. They also have a light-sensitive pineal gland. For the agnathans, reproduction and development are external. There is no known form of post-natal care. Some fish show the first vertebral column in their bodies, known as the notochord. They retain the notochord for the rest of their lives.

Jawless Fish

The two main types of jawless fish were the lampreys and the hagfish. They had unpaired fins and circular mouths. Their heart had two chambers and they were ectothermic in nature. It is uncertain if jawless fish lived in shallow, marine waters, or if the force of the freshwater streams washed their fossils towards shallow water streams.

▲ Devonian Doryaspis fish; Doryaspis is an extinct genus of primitive jawless fish that lived in the ocean during the Devonian Period

▲ Biologists say that sturgeon fish are the most primitive of the bony fish alive today

Feeding Habits of Agnathans

Since they are ectothermic, or cold-blooded, they eat little food and do not rely on a speedy metabolism to stay warm. The early jawless fish were soft-bodied. They fed on tiny organisms by the process of filter-feeding. Fish would prey on microorganisms at the bottom of the sea by sucking or nibbling from their mouths. The food would then be passed onto their large gill cavities, which also processed water and helped the fish breathe.

The gill cavities had very large surface areas to suit this purpose, and the gill apparatus would redirect the food to the canal. The gill, therefore, evolved to be multipurpose and took care of the eating and breathing needs of the fish. The head and gills were protected by a dermal armour, whereas their tails had unrestricted freedom of movement.

▲ Sharks are cartilaginous fish

Lampreys and Hagfish

These fish have interested evolutionary scientists because modern agnathans continue to possess primitive characteristics. This order also includes the oldest known craniate fossils. Lampreys and hagfish are modern agnathans.

 ## Lampreys

Lampreys and hagfish have the notochord. It is a circular, jawless mouth. Lampreys also have unpaired fins and eel-like scaleless skin. They have one or two dorsal fins, well-developed eyes, and teeth on their tongue, as well as an oral disc. Adult lampreys are sized between 35–60 centimetres. They also have an elongated larval stage. They breed in freshwater rivers, lakes, and ponds. This makes them **anadromous**, which means they migrate up from rivers to spawn in the sea.

▲ Some species of lampreys can be parasitic as they feed on the blood of other fish

▶ A lamprey has 7 gill pores on each side of the head

 ## Reproduction in Lampreys

When lampreys reproduce, they build a nest in the water, lay their eggs, and die after fertilisation. Their breeding period can last for 18 months. The larvae grow to a maximum size of 10 centimetres. There are 41 extant species of lampreys, out of which 18 are parasitic and 23 remain confined to freshwater habitats. They also exist in the ocean but prefer coastal regions. They are found in most temperate regions, with the exception of Africa. They are not tolerant of high water temperatures, and thus do not thrive in tropical environments. The landlocked lampreys are limited in size.

Reproduction in Hagfish

Hagfish usually inhabit high-saline waters and do not like direct exposure to light. Thus, they are found at the mouths of rivers or more than 1,000 metres below the ocean's surface. They are the only vertebrate whose body fluids are isosmotic with seawater and they are found only in marine waters. Their diets consist of dead fish and invertebrates. Like scavengers, they eat the insides of dying fish. They cannot directly penetrate the skin of their prey, so they enter natural openings such as the prey's mouth, gills, or anus. They do not have jaws, but instead have a pair of tooth-like projections that help pull up food. They do not primarily prey on fish and are themselves often consumed by seabirds and crustaceans. They have a very slow metabolism and only need to feed a few times in one month.

◀ As opposed to lampreys, hagfish do not have a larval stage

 ## Hagfish

Hagfish belong to the order Myxiniformes. They are known for their eel-like bodies. A fossil study of hagfish shows that their anatomies have remained unchanged for the past 300 million years! Their bodies are scaleless and they have unpaired fins, a single nostril, and paddle-like tails. They can be found in a range of colours from pink to blue-grey. Their teeth are located on their tongues, and they have degenerate eyes. On an average, they measure about 50 centimetres. Each hagfish has both the ovaries and the testes, but only one functional gonad.

🐾 In Real Life

An adult hagfish can secrete so much slime that it can turn a big bucket of water into thick gel within minutes. When held by the tail, the hagfish escapes by secreting a slime that becomes a thick gel when in contact with water. They clean themselves of this slime by tying themselves into an overhand knot and using it to scrape themselves from head to tail.

Bony v/s Cartilaginous Fish

A distinct feature of the fish evolution cycle was the early development of bone, cartilage, and enamel-like substance. This helped the fish adapt to diverse aquatic environments in the water and even on land.

 ## Differences

There are many differences between the bony fish and the cartilaginous fish. The most important difference is that the skeleton of the bony fish is made of bones, whereas the skeleton of cartilaginous fish is made of cartilage.

Features	Bony Fish	Cartilaginous Fish
Skeleton	The **endoskeleton** is made of bones. Their **exoskeleton** or external covering is made of cycloids (thin, bony plates).	The endoskeleton is made of cartilage. Their exoskeleton is made of placoid, that are small denticles with a sharp, enamel coating.
Mouth	They have an anterior tip mouth opening.	They have a ventral mouth.
Operculum	They have opercula on either side of the gills.	They do not have an operculum.
Tail	They have a homocercal tail fin.	They have a heterocercal tail fin.
Swim bladder	Also called an air bladder or buoyancy organ, it is present in most bony fish. It contains oxygen and allows the fish to maintain their depth without floating upwards or sinking.	It is absent in all cartilaginous fish and bottom-dwelling fish.
Habitat	They are found in both fresh water and marine water.	They are predominantly present in marine waters.
Reproduction	They externally fertilise their eggs.	The fertilisation is internal.
Excretion	They excrete ammonia.	They excrete urea.

 ## Flying Fish

The flying fish is a bony fish commonly found in warm seas. They consume a variety of small creatures, but mainly plankton and measure 17–30 centimetres in length. These fish have pectoral fins that are like a bird's wings. They use these fins to easily glide over water. They usually swim in schools and consist of over 40 different types of oceanic fish. Some species such as the blue flying fish have two wings, whereas some are four-winged, like the California flying fish. They are preyed on by dolphins, tuna, and mackerel. They avoid these predators with their aerial skills.

▲ *Illustration of the flying fish*

Flying fish do not generally fly, but rather glide on their fins at the speed of about 59 kmph. They can easily cover a distance of 200 metres. The flying fish build up speed under water, then become airborne, making many consecutive glides with their tails propelling their movement above water. The strong fliers can even go as fast as around 400 metres in one single glide!

◄ *On an average, flying fish live up to 5 years*

Dogfish

Dogfish is an example of a cartilaginous fish. It travels in a dense school of fish and preys on other fish and invertebrates. The spiny shark has a sharp spine in front of each of its two dorsal fins. The dorsal fins have venom glands that can cause painful injuries. It is between 60–140 centimetres long. People kill dogfish for food or to produce shark liver oil. They have also been used to make fertilisers.

▲ *Dogfish have been considered a nuisance because they end up ripping fishnets after taking bait*

Predatory Sharks

Sharks—for some, hearing the word itself sends chills down the spine. In reality, most sharks do not attack humans unless they feel threatened. However, human beings hunt sharks for their fins, teeth, meat, and skin. So human beings do pose a threat to their survival. There are over 500 species of sharks in this world today.

 ## Behaviour and Intelligence

Although considered to be instinct-driven hunters, many species of sharks have exhibited complex problem-solving skills and high curiosity. They have also shown signs of playful behaviour by repeatedly rolling around in kelp and chasing a trail in the ocean for fun. If a shark feels threatened, it exhibits exaggerated swimming movements to ward off predators. The intensity of the movements is directly dependent on how threatened the shark feels.

 ## Sleep Patterns

Some sharks sleep like dolphins, with one part of their brain active and awake, while the rest of the brain rests. Some sharks use their spiracles to continue swimming while they sleep. Their spinal cord coordinates the activity of swimming so that the brain can rest. Some sink to the bottom of the ocean and lie still with their eyes open and actively pump water over their gills.

▲ *A scuba diver is seen swimming with the whale shark. These sharks are harmless, but they can be spooked by too much movement or artificial light*

▶ *There are 10 different species of hammerhead sharks. They vary in size but have the same basic features*

Hammerhead Sharks

Hammerhead sharks are cartilaginous animals. Each hammerhead shark is 13–20 feet in length and weighs anywhere between 230 and 450 kilograms. What makes this shark unique is the shape of its head, which looks like a flattened hammer. With this peculiar shape, the hammerhead shark can lift and turn its head quickly.

Their wide-set eyes give them a wider view of the surroundings. The hammerhead sharks have expanded nostrils, thereby giving them a better sense of smell and better ability to locate the prey than other fish. Moreover, the underside of the wide head has **electroreceptive organs**, which help these sharks detect the electrical impulses given off by their prey. Great hammerhead sharks are greyish brown or olive green on top, with a white underside.

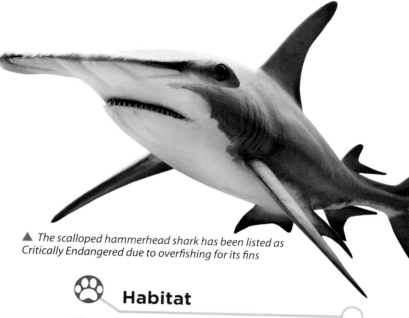

▲ *The scalloped hammerhead shark has been listed as Critically Endangered due to overfishing for its fins*

Hunting

The great hammerhead is the largest of the 10 identified species of this shark. It has sharp, blade-like teeth. It preys on larger fish, squids, crabs, smaller sharks, and its favourite, the stingrays. As a matter of fact, the shark uses its electroreceptive organs to hunt for stingrays, which usually bury themselves under sand. They use their enormous heads to hold the stingrays down during a fight.

Habitat

The sharks are present in tropic or temperate marine waters. They feed around shallow coastal areas, estuaries, and salty waters. In winters, huge schools of hammerhead sharks are seen migrating towards the warmth of the equator and in summer they move towards the poles.

Young Ones

All species of hammerhead sharks are viviparous, which means that the females retain fertilised eggs within their bodies to give birth to live young ones. The female great hammerhead shark gives birth to several dozens of young ones at a time. The females give birth in shallow waters in summer and spring. The young ones continue to stay there until they are old enough to venture into the oceans.

▶ *Sharks have been around for more than 400 million years*

The True Eels

Eels belong to the order Anguilliformes and are known as teleost fish. The most famous types of eels are the common freshwater eels and aggressive marine morays.

▲ *A group of electric eels swimming together in an aquarium*

Life as an Eel

Eels are known for their elongated, wormlike bodies and characterised by the absence of pelvic fins (fins on the bottom of the body) and scales that are usually found in other fish families. Almost all eels are found in marine (saltwater) habitats with an interesting exception being the freshwater eel. Even though this eel lives in freshwater rivers and lakes, it travels to a marine environment to spawn, and the young eels then travel back to the fresh water. This phenomenon makes the freshwater eels **catadromous**.

The name 'eel' has been applied to species of different orders as well. Some examples are electric eels, bobtail snipe eels, swamp eels, and spiny eels. However, 'true eels' belong to the order Anguilliformes. These animals have made a significant contribution to the ecosystems they are part of and to human beings as well. In food chains, they are predators of other fish and invertebrates such as molluscs and crustaceans. Eels have also become a delicacy in many parts of the world.

Appearance

Eels vary in size according to their species. They range from 10 cm to 3 m in length and can weigh more than 65 kg. The conger eel is the largest in the eel family, reaching 3 m in length. An adult conger eel weighs around 110 kg.

Social Behaviour

Eels often live in groups in individual holes called eel pits, with only certain species such as the electric eel living in solitary conditions. These pits are found in shallow waters or in the bottom layer of the ocean. Some eels adapt to deeper waters and reach depths of 4,000 metres. Other eels are active swimmers and remain approximately 500 metres below the surface.

▲ *The European eel is critically endangered according to the IUCN*

Eels and Human Beings

Different species of eels are used as food in different parts of the world. Even though raw eel blood is toxic to human beings, the toxins are neutralised while cooking. The most commonly known culinary use of eel is seen in Japanese food. Freshwater eels are known as unagi and marine eels are known as anago. Jellied eels are a tradition in London and eels from the Comacchio area, in Italy, are a speciality. Eels are also often used for entertainment. In the USA, moray eels are widely used in tropical saltwater aquariums.

▲ *Though there are many species of eels present in water, there is a specific type of eel used in different cuisines*

▲ *Kabayaki is a dish prepared in Japanese cuisine. It is made with an unagi eel. The dish has different methods of preparation*

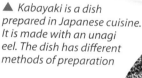

▶ *It is easy to distinguish between other eels and the moray eel because of its drastically different appearance*

▲ *An eel is seen moving on dead patch reefs. These provide shelter to eels*

Moray Eels

Moray eels are seen around the world. There are 200 species of these eels found in the oceans and seas. Most of the species are seen in brackish waters; only some prefer fresh water. So, these eels are found in both freshwater and saltwater habitats.

The moray eels living in tropical climates live in coral rubble rocks, dead patch reefs, and coral reefs. They are located near the equator. The reason that these eels have long bodies is that they have more vertebrae. Unlike in other eels, the moray eels have vertebrae between the pre-tail and tail regions of their bodies. They are carnivorous animals who attack and eat cuttlefish, barracudas, groupers, octopuses, and sea snakes.

Incredible Individuals

Alexander von Humboldt (1769–1859) was a naturalist from Germany. For some reason, he set out in search of some electric eels while he was travelling in South America. He asked some people to help him catch electric eels that were at least 2 metres in length. Surprisingly, they made around 30 horses charge into the water. The surprised eels jumped out of the water and sent shocks through the horses in defence. Once they were tired out, the men collected the eels and provided them to Humboldt. He then wrote about the incident of the 'jumping' electric eels.

▲ *He was the first to connect altitude sickness to a lack of oxygen*

Skates and Ratfish

Skates and ratfish are cartilaginous fish. They are related to the shark family, but their appearances vary greatly.

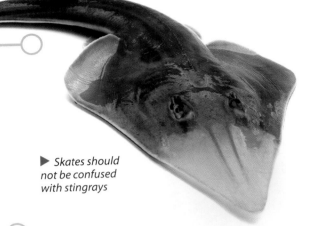

Skates

Skates are very interesting-looking marine animals that belong to the order Rajiformes. They have enlarged pectoral fins that extend from the snout to the base of the tail. Typically, skates have two dorsal fins and their mouth and gills are located in the bottom section of their bodies. They have sharp noses and solid or patterned coats. Skates can vary in size according to their species. The common skate can reach up to 2.8 metres, while the little skate is just 50 centimetres long.

▶ *Skates should not be confused with stingrays*

Features of Skates

Skates inhabit oceans all around the world, from the Arctic to the Antarctic waters. They are benthic, which means that they are found partially buried in the bottom of the ocean. They are very graceful swimmers. They are carnivores and prey aerially on fish, molluscs, and crustaceans. Skates have very low reproductive rates and lay eggs. Their eggs are popularly called 'mermaid's purse' because they are found ashore and are protected by a leathery capsule-like case. In 2006, they were named as a critically endangered species by the IUCN.

▲ *Skates have been in existence since the Jurassic period*

Ratfish

Ratfish, also known as chimaera, belong to the subclass Holocephali, class Chondrichthyes and are related to the well-feared sharks. They are scaleless and are sized between 0.3-1.2 metres in length. They have projecting snouts, ventral mouths, large pectoral and pelvic fins, and very large eyes. They have two dorsal fins that are fronted with poisonous glands. They also have a sharp spine and large, wing-like pectoral fins. Their coats can be of a range of silvery to blackish colours. Like rats, they have slender tails, a prominent feature after which they have been named.

▲ *Ratfish's swim is often termed as aquatic flight due to its resemblance to a bird*

Features of Ratfish

Ratfish are found in temperate or cold waters in diverse marine habitats. They are not agile swimmers, which makes them an easy target for predators. Ratfish feed on small fish, molluscs, and crustaceans. They use their strong teeth to grind their prey. When ratfish reproduce, their females lay eggs that are protected by sharp coverings. These fish are hunted because they are edible and considered to be delicious. They are also killed for the liver oil they produce, which is used as a lubricant for guns and other such instruments.

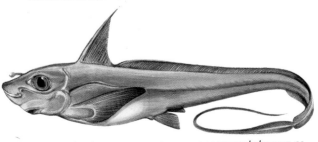

▲ *Chimaera monstrosa are commonly known as rabbit fish or ratfish*

The Unique Swordfish

Swordfish are large ocean fish. Their distinctive feature is their long flat bill, which bears a close resemblance to a sword, therefore awarding them the nomenclature of swordfish or broadbill.

Appearance

They are elongated, scaleless fish with a tall dorsal fin. They use their long snout to slash at their prey. The 'sword' is flat, rather than rounded as in marlins. Marlins and swordfish belong to the same family along with other spear-nosed fish. The bodies of swordfish are very large, known to grow up to the length of about 4.6 metres. They can weigh about 650 kilograms. They have a distinctive purplish or bluish coat on the top which blends into a silvery and white coat near the underside. So they can blend in well near the surface of the water as well as with what is found living below them. The swordfish is also distinguished by its lack of pelvic fins and teeth.

Swordfish are incapable of maintaining a body temperature higher than the temperature of the surrounding waters. Instead, they have unique muscle and brown tissue that warms blood flowing to the brain and eyes, enabling them to tolerate the extreme cold of the ocean's depths. This is what gives them the sharp eyesight that proves fundamental to their survival at various stages.

 The blue marlin swordfish is one of 12 species

Social Behaviour

Swordfish are isolated fish and they do not form schools; but they look for food with the others in a group. They are often sighted near the surface of the water engaging in an activity called 'breaching', where they are seen jumping out of the water. They are one of the fastest animals in the ocean, moving at a speed of 80 kmph. This affords them a significant advantage over their prey. The prey mostly consists of fish such as rockfish, the barracuda, and molluscs such as squids. They possess an enormous appetite owing to their size and are known to hunt actively at night. In the case of swordfish, conception is an external process where the female releases eggs into the open ocean and the male secretes sperm, leading to fertilisation.

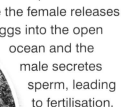

 From the fertilised eggs, swordfish hatch as larvae. They are 4 millimetres in length

Migration

Though they are found at various depths in the ocean, swordfish are known to migrate through warm and cold waters depending on the season. They tend to stick to warmer waters. The majority of them are found in the Pacific Ocean. They tend to migrate a great deal in order to find food and to be able to stay in the warmer areas of the water. They also go back to cooler waters in the summer to avoid getting too hot. Ideally, they want water that is between 17–21° C.

Current State

Swordfish have few predators. These include human beings, large sharks, and killer whales. Their numbers have always faced the highest threat from human beings. The start of the century had seen a threat to the existence of swordfish because of the popularity and demand for it at restaurants. The IUCN took notice and started working on curbing the rapid decline of the swordfish population.

The Smooth Rays

Rays are the closest relatives of sharks. There are 600 odd species of these fish, the most famous being the stingrays. The eagle ray, the mobula ray, the blue-spotted ray, and the manta ray are some other species.

Body Type

Stingrays have flat bodies that look wide due to the fact that their fins extend to both extremities of their bodies from head to trunk. Their bodies are supported by cartilage instead of bones, just like their shark relatives. They defend themselves with their tails, which have jagged edges and long spines on them. Some stingrays even carry a dangerous venom in their tails.

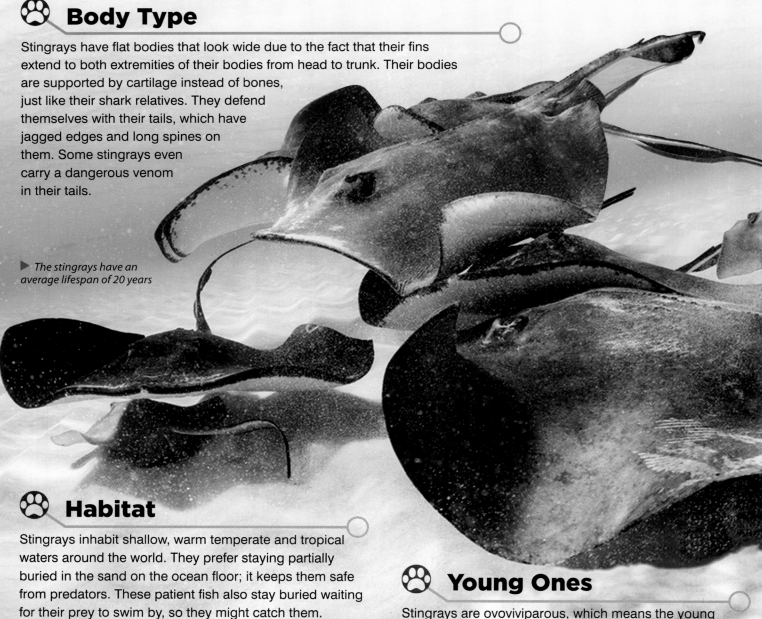

▶ The stingrays have an average lifespan of 20 years

Habitat

Stingrays inhabit shallow, warm temperate and tropical waters around the world. They prefer staying partially buried in the sand on the ocean floor; it keeps them safe from predators. These patient fish also stay buried waiting for their prey to swim by, so they might catch them. Stingrays eat mussels, oysters, crabs, and shrimps, which they crush with their jaws.

Deadly Stingrays

Most stingrays swim by moving their entire body in a wave, which propels them forward. If one happened to step onto a stingray, it would lash at them with its tail, causing deadly wounds. Some human beings have even died during such accidents. If you want to avoid stepping on a stingray, just move your feet quickly in a shuffling motion. These movements will cause vibrations that can alert the stingrays to back off.

Young Ones

Stingrays are ovoviviparous, which means the young ones are hatched from eggs held within the female's body. Females give birth once a year to 2–6 young ones at a time. The offspring are fully developed within the mother's body, so they look developed when born, ready to lead independent lives.

Senses

The mouth, nostrils, and gills are located on the underside of the stingray, while its eyes are on the top. Scientists believe that the eyes do not help them much in hunting, but they have special sensors which help them detect electric charges emitted by the prey they are hunting.

Freshwater v/s Saltwater

Fish have been in existence for more than 450 million years. They have repeatedly evolved to fit into almost every conceivable type of aquatic habitat. The general idea of a fish can often be misleading as there are over 30,000 species of fish and their shapes and structures vary drastically.

Habitat

Fish inhabit two broad types of habitats. They are the freshwater and saltwater habitats. Marine habitats can be divided into deep ocean floors (benthic), mid-water oceanic (bathypelagic), surface oceanic (pelagic), rocky coast, sandy coast, muddy shores, bays, estuaries, and others. Current human knowledge is limited to their geographical distribution and not the origin of said distribution.

Types of Freshwater Fish

Freshwater fish have been classified as warm-water, cool-water and cold-water. Catfish are warm-water fish who like the water to be around 27° C in temperature.

Perch and walleye prefer cool water, with an average temperature of 16° C to 27° C, while cold-water fish such as trout prefer low temperatures between 10°C to 16°C.

▶ *Catfish are ray-finned fish. They are called 'catfish' because of the cat-like whiskers seen around their mouth*

Types of Saltwater Fish

From the fossils collected over the years, palaeontologists have classified saltwater fish into the three categories—Agnatha, Chondrichthyes, and Osteichthyes.

Order Agnatha refers to a type of jawless fish having a circular mouth with rings of teeth. Hagfish and lampreys are the two types of agnathans.

Order Chondrichthyes consists of sharks and stingrays. We can trace their origin to the Jurassic Era, about 200 million years ago.

Order Osteichthyes consists of bony fish. These are the most common type of fish, with over 23,000 species belonging to this order.

▲ *Fish can also drown when there is a lack of oxygen in the water*

How Fish Choose Their Habitats

How is it that some fish prefer freshwater habitats and others prefer saltwater habitats? Fish prefer habitats that provide opportunities for mating, plenty of food, and have few predators. There is another factor that affects their choice of habitats. It is the salinity of the water.

Freshwater fish can survive in salt-deficient waters. In fact, they have developed certain physiological mechanisms that allow them to concentrate salts within their own bodies in the freshwater habitats. Saltwater fish, on the other hand, excrete salts. But the few fish that can live in both habitats have developed various mechanisms to deal with the differences between the two.

The Ferocious Piranhas

Piranhas have a very nasty reputation among human beings. People believe that they can bite or attack people in groups. This is because of incorrect portrayals in movies. Though piranhas can be fierce and fearsome, there are very few reports of them actually biting human beings.

 ## Species

There are 20 confirmed species of piranhas living in South America. They are freshwater fish found in rivers and lakes. Among them, the black piranha is the largest. It follows a carnivorous diet. Other species, like the red-bellied piranha, follow an omnivorous diet.

Behaviour

Piranhas are often seen swimming in groups as this is the best way to protect themselves from predators. When they feel threatened, they warn their enemies to leave them alone by 'barking'. They only bite when the attacker continues to annoy them. They feed on small shrimps, worms, and even molluscs. Once it sees a prey, a piranha will swim closer to it and open its mouth wide. Inside its mouth, it has triangle-shaped teeth. They are extremely sharp. A piranha can open up its mouth and gobble up smaller shrimps or molluscs in one quick gulp! Schools of piranhas can contain around 100 individuals. Each piranha can grow to 35 centimetres in size.

▲ *Red-bellied piranha are sometimes kept as aquarium fish*

▲ *Black-bellied piranha piranhas can bite with a force three times their own body weight*

▼ *The red-bellied piranhas are typically found in white water rivers such as the Amazon River Basin*

A Poisonous Defence

Whether they live in the ocean or a large aquarium, fish make the world beautiful. They are also great at defending themselves against predators. Quite a few of these creatures have defence mechanisms that could harm not just their predators, but also human beings.

Sting like a Stonefish

A stonefish is about 30 centimetres in length, with a large head and mouth, and small eyes. These details sound ordinary, but the fish is extraordinary. It carries venom in its skin and in sacs attached to the razor-sharp spines along its back.

When attacked or accidentally stepped onto, the stonefish pushes the spines into the predator and releases the poison. The sting of the spine can lead to paralysis or even death in a few cases. These fish are bottom-dwellers; they live in estuaries, rocks, or in the corals found in the world's oceans.

▶ *A stonefish uses the rocks and corals of its surroundings as camouflage*

All Puffed Up

Pufferfish, also known as blowfish, have the amazing ability to expand. They swim clumsily, making them an easy target for predators. But to escape, the fish fill their elastic stomach with water, and at times air, to become an inedible ball several times larger than their size. Some species of pufferfish have spines on them, making them even less palatable.

The next line of defence the pufferfish use is tetrodotoxin, a deadly toxin present in almost all 120 species of pufferfish. It is so lethal that the predators, including humans, barely stand a chance for survival. There is enough poison in a single pufferfish to kill almost 30 adult human beings. There is no **antidote** available to fight the toxin.

▲ *The only species immune to pufferfish toxin are sharks*

Fatal Red

The average length of a red lionfish is about one foot. It lives amongst the rocks and crevices of the Indian Ocean and the Pacific Ocean, but it has been introduced to warm waters worldwide. The red lionfish looks striking with brown, red, and white stripes.

It has around 18 venom-filled, needle-shaped dorsal fins. If disturbed, it spreads its fins and if further intimidated, it attacks. If a human being is attacked by the sting of the red lionfish, they might feel nauseous and would not be able to tolerate the pain, but it is rarely fatal.

◀ *The red lionfish is a prized aquarium fish*

The King Salmon

Chinook salmon, or the king salmon, are the largest of the salmon species found in the Pacific. They can grow up to almost 3 feet in length. They live in the cold waters of the upper reaches of the Pacific Ocean in countries such as the United States of America and Canada. Chinook salmon can be found even in Russia and Japan.

A Dual Life

Chinook salmon are **anadromous** fish, which means they can live in fresh water as well as the salty ocean waters. Their life cycle starts and ends in fresh water. They spend their early years in the ocean as they can eat plenty of food and thrive in the open waters.

Eggs

The process of reproduction begins when the Chinook salmon migrate to their breeding grounds. The female digs a small hole in the sandy bottom of a freshwater river or stream. This is like a nest and is called redd. This is where the eggs are laid. A Chinook salmon can lay about 1,000 eggs at one time.

▲ *These fish hatch in freshwater but spend their adult lives at sea*

The eggs laid by the female are fertilised by the male salmon. Both guard eggs from predators. The eggs stay put until the embryo develops. These salmon spend so much energy on travelling to the breeding grounds and protecting the eggs that they die even before the eggs can hatch.

▲ *When Chinook salmon swim upstream for spawning, they often become food for grizzly bears*

▶ *Chinook salmon are blue-green on the head and back, and silver on the sides. They change colour when moving to fresh water. During the mating season, both male and female Chinook salmon display a slight shade of red on the tail and fins*

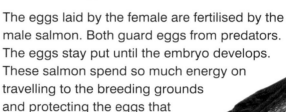

Alevins

On complete development, the embryo spins inside the egg until it hatches, after which the babies are released. These baby salmon are called **alevins**. The alevins stay near the nest. They have a yolk sac attached to themselves. They take their nourishment from there and grow. They continue to do so until they learn to find their own food.

Fry

Once the fish finish feeding from the yolk sac and grow, they move from the nest. The baby salmon without the yolk sac are called the fry. The fry leave the nest and move to the surface of the water. They continue to live in the fresh water until they are ready to move to the sea.

The amount of time spent by the fry varies amongst different species of salmon. Chinook fry spend less than five months in fresh water. They keep themselves safe by hiding behind boulders and logs.

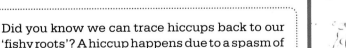

▶ *The populations of the Chinook salmon fish are declining in some places such as California, USA; in other places they are thriving*

Smolt

At this stage, the fry is big enough to move towards the ocean. The fish continue to grow. The face, jaw and scales are much larger now. Their bodies become long, elongated and silvery in a process called smolting.

The smolts continue to grow as they move towards the estuary. Here they get a mix of fresh and salty water, helping them adjust to the presence of salt. They feed to grow and survive in the ocean.

Open Waters

The Chinook salmon can spend up to eight years in sea water. They are then ready to migrate back to the stream where they were born. This is what makes the life cycle of salmon so interesting. All species of salmon, including Chinooks, swim against the tide and move upstream to complete their goal of laying and fertilising eggs in their original homes. It is said that the chemicals released by their bodies help them adapt to these changing environments of fresh water and salty water.

💡 Isn't It Amazing!

Did you know we can trace hiccups back to our 'fishy roots'? A hiccup happens due to a spasm of the diaphragm and is followed by an involuntary gulp. Originally, for fish, breathing was a process involving the brain, throat, and gills. In human beings, the process includes the throat, the chest, and the diaphragm, and sometimes, this complex arrangement can spasm our nerves, resulting in a hiccup! Once we begin to hiccup, it is kept going by a motor reflex seen in ancient tadpoles. It helped them direct water only to their gills, but is not useful for us. However, it does shed some light on our common ancestry.

Full Circle

If not eaten by bears and other predators, the salmon will safely reach home. There, once again, like their parents, they will lay eggs and fertilise them. During the journey, the salmon rely on their surroundings, the sun, and scents to reach their destination.

Hooked noses on the males help them fight others so that they can win over a female and mate with her. The females lay eggs in the redd, which they form by pushing aside small rocks.

Portuguese Man O' War

This interesting-sounding animal gets its name from its uppermost part, which sits above water and resembles a Portuguese sailing warship at full sail. It is also called Floating Terror. Let us take a look at this creature that is often wrongly thought to be a jellyfish.

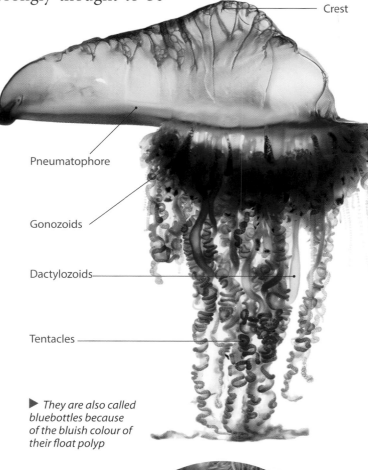

Crest

Pneumatophore

Gonozoids

Dactylozoids

Tentacles

▶ *They are also called bluebottles because of the bluish colour of their float polyp*

Full Blown Sail

The Portuguese man o' war is about three metres long. It has tentacles which can reach a massive length of almost 50 metres. It is found in warm oceanic waters around the world. The Portuguese man o' war is a cousin of the jellyfish. It is an interesting animal. It appears to be a single organism, but in reality, it is a colony of hundreds of hydra-like individuals. These are called polyps and they work in perfect tandem.

▲ *The Portuguese man o' war has a beautiful shape and colour, but you should not approach it as it can sting you*

Polyps

The polyps are divided into four types based on the functions they perform. The uppermost polyp is the float polyp, and gives the organism its unique name. It is a gas-filled chamber and is also known as pneumatophore.

A man o' war simply moves with the oceanic currents. If it feels threatened, the float polyp deflates to submerge for a short while.

The next are the tentacles or the dactylozooids, also known as the stinging polyps. They are covered with poison-filled cells called nematocysts, which paralyse and kill fish and other small marine creatures. Man o' war is not fatal to humans but can cause a sting that may take weeks to heal.

It is the feeding polyps or gastrozooids which actually work on the prey. The last are the reproductive polyp or gonozooids. As the name suggests, they perform the function of reproduction.

▶ *A cluster of Portuguese man o' war, with the tops of their heads visible*

⊙ Incredible Individuals

Ever wonder where the names of different animals come from? William Elford Leach often named animals after people he knew. He named nine species in his lifetime, including several crustaceans. He named many species after an unknown woman named Caroline. He also named some after his friend John Cranch.

Soft-bodied Molluscs

Molluscs are highly adaptive soft-bodied invertebrate species from the phylum Mollusca. They are wholly or partially enclosed in a protective calcium carbonate shell secreted by the soft mantle which also covers their body. These are one of the most diverse groups in the animal kingdom alongside insects and vertebrates, with the possibility of 150,000 identified and unidentified species. There is immense ecological and structural variety in each group of molluscs.

Order

Molluscs are classified into nine different groups, out of which two have been designated as extinct. These are wormlike organisms or Solenogastres; chitons or Polyplacophora; cap-shelled molluscs or Monoplacophora; slugs and snails or Gastropoda; hard-shelled organisms like clams or Bivalvia; tusk-shelled organisms or Scaphopoda; squid or Cephalopoda; Rostroconchia (extinct); and Helcionelloida (extinct).

Adaptability

Molluscs are proven to be highly adaptive as they have evolved into species that are present everywhere in nature, except air. Bivalves, gastropods, and cephalopods are usually seen in a marine environment but there are some species of gastropods that have successfully evolved and adapted themselves to land, with thousands of species existing terrestrially, taking advantage of sandy and muddy substrates to crawl, burrow, or to cement themselves to these surfaces.

▲ *Shelled molluscs have powerful muscles called 'adductors', which help them shut the shell quickly to avoid predators*

Clams

Clams are found in shallow waters, in which they are protected by water currents and also because they have a cemented grip where they burrow or traverse over. They have shells that they open or close using their two adductor muscles. Certain species of Bivalvia clam have been discovered in the Pacific Ocean at a depth of more than 4,800 metres. The size of clams ranges from 0.1 millimetres in condylocardia to 1.2 metres in the giant clam of the Pacific and Indian Oceans.

◀ *A collection of clamshells*

Feeding and Survival

Clams draw in and expel water for the purpose of feeding and respiration through two separate tubes which are also called the siphons or 'neck'. This process helps accumulate food strained from the ongoing water currents, which is then transported to the mouth entangled in mucus. A few species of clams do not feed in the normal sense; they gain their nutrition from sulphur-oxidising bacteria that live symbiotically in the gill tissue. They are commonly found at marine hydrothermal vents and in sulphide-rich sediments.

💡 Isn't It Amazing!

Clams are an interesting and diverse species. A few clams, such as the gem clam, have internal fertilisation and development. There are clams or shell-based molluscs which produce the pearls we use as jewellery. Disco clams are known for putting on a show with reflected light.

Spectacular Tentacles

Octopuses are molluscs. They are called cephalopods, which means 'head-footed'. Unlike snails, in case of octopuses, their molluscan foot is located at the headend. The animal is named octopus because of the eight distinct arms of the invertebrate.

Facts of Physique

Octopuses have soft, round, sac-like bodies. They have large bulging eyes and a beak-like mouth hidden in the ring of arms. The powerful arms are covered with suction cups called suckers. These are used to catch prey, move over rocks, and swim.

An interesting fact about this invertebrate is that it has three hearts and nine brains. Two of its hearts supply blood to the gills, the breathing organ. The third heart is the organ heart, which supplies blood to the other organs.

▲ *Female octopus have to keep their eggs safe from predators as well as gently guide currents of water over them, so that they get a fresh supply of oxygen. They do this without leaving their side or eating. When the eggs hatch, the mother is so exhausted and starved, that she dies*

Blue-blooded

The blood of an octopus is blue in colour because of the presence of hemocyanin, a copper-rich protein. This protein binds to the oxygen molecules, thus helping transport oxygen throughout the body.

▲ *On mating, the female octopuses lay eggs on rocks. They are small, shaped like a teardrop and milky in appearance*

Intelligent Beings

Octopus brains are another story. One of them, the big one, controls the **nervous system**, while the remaining small brains control the animal's tentacles. Long ago, octopuses were thought to be dumb, but did you know they are one of the most intelligent invertebrates? They are known to recognise different colours, shapes, carry out simple tasks such as opening boxes, navigate through mazes, and solve simple problems.

Dwelling and Feeding

Octopuses are solitary creatures. They build dens with rocks that they move with their arms. Few do live near the water's surface, but most octopuses are deep-sea dwellers. They crawl on the ocean floors using their arms, looking for food to eat. They rise at dawn and dusk to look for food along the water's surface. Their favourite meals include crabs, shrimps, and lobsters.

Camouflage

Octopuses have pigment cells and special muscles which help them not just change colours but also match the texture and pattern of their surroundings. Sharks, dolphins and many other predators simply swim past such a camouflaged octopus.

Defence

If a camouflaged octopus is discovered, it squirts an ink-like liquid. This darkens the surrounding water, dulling the predator's sense of smell, giving the octopus enough time to escape. If this fails too and the octopus is caught by the predator by its arm, it just lets go the body part. Yes, it can regrow its arm! The beak-like mouth can also give a nasty bite to the predator and the saliva too is filled with venom.

Sticky Barnacles

If you own a ship, you might be familiar with barnacles. They are notorious for sticking to the bottom of a vessel, requiring the cleaner to use a lot of energy to get rid of them. Barnacles are crustaceans who live in the water.

 ## Behaviour

Barnacles belong to the subclass Cirripedia. They live a sedentary life, which means that they stay in the same place for a long time. There are 850 species of marine barnacles and 260 species that act as parasites. They live in crustaceans like crabs.

Barnacles are covered with plates made of calcium carbonate. These are their **calcareous** plates. They choose different surfaces to stay on, but prefer places that are very active, such as an underwater volcano or the bottom of a ship, the bodies of whales and other larger animals, seaweed, rocks, and clams. They stick to these surfaces by releasing a fast-curing cement. It is such an efficient and sticky glue that researchers are trying to figure out how it can be used by humans.

 ## Feeding Habits

Barnacles eat from their appendages. These are called cirri and look like little feathers. There is an opening on the barnacle from which the cirri reach out for food and retract. They eat microscopic organisms.

Many barnacles are circled by six calcareous plates and four more that behave like a door, opening and closing when the tide comes in and out. They close the door to conserve moisture and open it to look for food. Barnacles are also seen as a delicacy in some cultures. The Japanese use goose barnacles in their cooking, and so do the Spanish and Portuguese. Picoroco barnacle is used in Chile.

In Real Life

Barnacles are **hermaphrodites.** It means that they possess both male and female reproductive organs. Some species might cross-fertilise while others fertilise themselves. Barnacles reproduce around six times a year. In cross-fertilisation, another barnacle might release sperm from a retractable tube that enters 6–8 inches into the partner's shell.

▲ Barnacles live for 8-20 years

▲ Barnacles are free-floating, but eventually attach themselves to rocks, shell, or other objects

▼ The gooseneck barnacle resembles the fleshy stalk in the region of the goose's neck. This led ancient people to believe that the geese grew from the goose barnacle

Floating Sea Otters

Not to be confused with otters, sea otters are marine animals. They are seen in the Pacific Ocean in North America and also in Asia. While they might spend their entire day in the water, some sleep on the shore. Their nostrils and ears have adapted to close when they are in water.

Otter Behaviour

Sea otters are often photographed floating on their backs on the surface of the water. They look like they are happily resting. Often, they float in a group or pair. They look for kelp forests and seaweed to use as an anchor in moving waters.

While they are floating, sea otters hold on their chests the rocks that they found ashore. They repeatedly hit the shellfish they have collected against the rocks to break them open and eat what is inside. They eat crabs, fish, octopuses, and sea urchins in the same way.

▲ Sea otters can remain submerged in water for over 5 minutes

On Their Backs

It seems as if sea otters do everything on their backs. They give birth in the water. Then, the mother otter cares for her young, while they are both on their backs. To feed their babies, they hold the infants against their chests. Sea otters learn to hunt for food and swim while they are still growing.

An adult sea otter grows to be 100–160 centimetres in length. It weighs 16–40 kilograms. They have slightly red or dark brown coats. These coats are valuable to human beings, so much so that sea otters almost went extinct because of how much they were hunted for their fur. While various countries made the effort to protect and conserve them, unfortunately, their numbers continue to decrease.

▲ A sea otter breaking apart a crab shell

◀ Sea otters have the thickest fur of any animal

☀ Isn't It Amazing!

Sea otters always keep their fur clean. This is important as their fur repels water, keeping them dry and warm. Like human beings, they wash themselves after a meal. They rub the water into the coat using their paws and teeth.

▼ Sea otters hold their food with their hands and collect it on their stomachs as they float

The Whiskered Walruses

Walruses are mammals, but they are considered marine animals. This is because they spend most of their lives in or around the sea. Walruses are commonly seen near the Arctic Circle. They are accompanied by hundreds of their own kind.

Bodies

Walruses have bulky bodies with blubber. This blubber allows them to stay warm and comfortable in the harsh, cold Arctic climate. Walruses can slow their heartbeats to lower their temperatures when they are swimming in the cool waters.

Species

Walruses have two main species. One species is the Atlantic walrus that lives in the coastal regions of Greenland and Canada. The other species is the Pacific walrus that lives in Russia and Alaska. It migrates from the Bering Sea to the Chukchi Sea.

▲ Walruses can live up to 40 years

Tusks

Walruses have tusks and hair around their face that looks like a moustache. They use these tusks to lift themselves out of the cold Arctic waters. They seemingly walk using their tusks and use them to break small holes into the ice. These are called breathing holes. All walruses have tusks, regardless of their sex. They do not stop growing and even act as canine teeth. A regular tusk can grow up to 1 metre in length.

Whiskers

Walruses have sensitive whiskers. They use these whiskers to find food like clams and shellfish when they are swimming in the ocean. They might swim all the way down to a darker, deeper part of the ocean for food, at which time their whiskers are more important than their eyesight for navigation.

▼ A close-up shot of a walrus' tusks. Its whiskers are about as sensitive as a person's fingers

Walruses and Climate Change

As walruses live near icy regions, they are greatly affected by climate change. There is a big population of walruses in the Chukchi Sea of the Arctic Ocean. The ice in this sea has started melting and continues to melt at an alarming rate. As there is a change in the distribution of ice in the sea, the walruses' diet, movement, and mating habits are changing. Their population is slowly reducing. They are forced to change where they forage for food during autumn and summer.

In the past, the number of walruses was in decline due to hunting. They were hunted for their tusks, skin, meat, oil, and so on during the 18th and 19th centuries. They nearly faced extinction. After changes in laws, only certain local tribes are allowed to hunt for walruses.

Homely Habitats

Almost all organisms on this planet have homes. There are places that fish and amphibians inhabit because it suits their lifestyles the best. These habitats provide them with food, water, and shelter as per their needs. Let us take a look at some of these interesting places that are home for various marine animals, and some animals that make unique use of their environments.

Coral Reefs

Coral reefs are not only home to corals, but also to seahorses, clownfish, sea turtles, etc. Corals themselves are marine animals. They have small tentacle-like arms that allow them to eat food, such as plankton, from the water. Similar to the coral reefs are the kelp forests, another major home for marine animals. Sea lions, whales, and other marine animals eat the small critters that live in the leaves found in abundance here. On the other hand, marine animals like crabs and oysters live in estuaries.

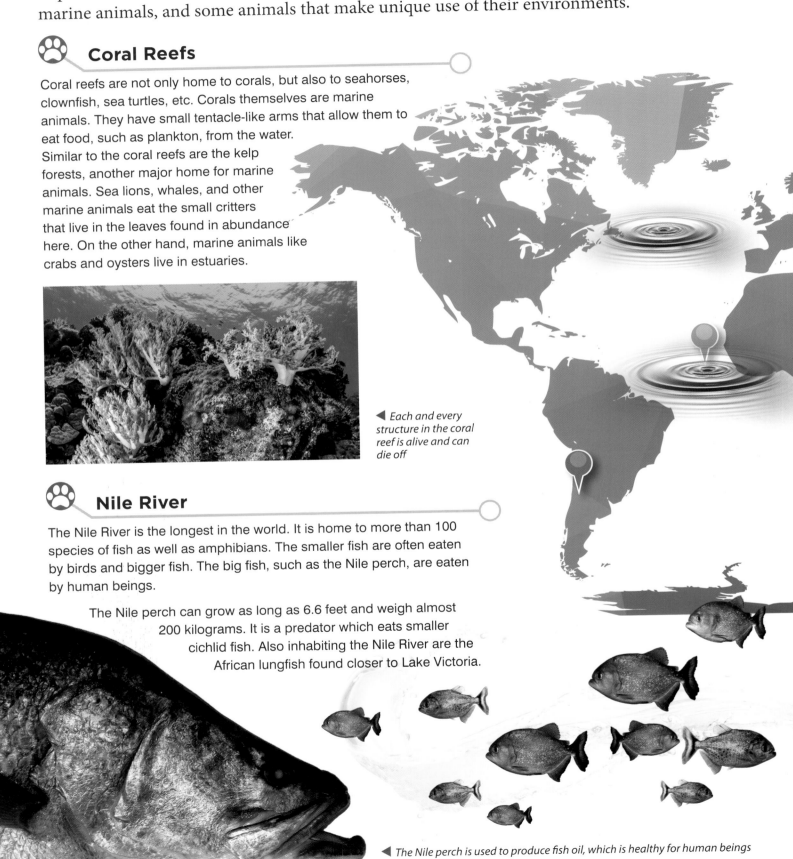

◄ Each and every structure in the coral reef is alive and can die off

Nile River

The Nile River is the longest in the world. It is home to more than 100 species of fish as well as amphibians. The smaller fish are often eaten by birds and bigger fish. The big fish, such as the Nile perch, are eaten by human beings.

The Nile perch can grow as long as 6.6 feet and weigh almost 200 kilograms. It is a predator which eats smaller cichlid fish. Also inhabiting the Nile River are the African lungfish found closer to Lake Victoria.

◄ The Nile perch is used to produce fish oil, which is healthy for human beings

Mudbanks

Lungfish, like the name suggests, have one or two lungs along with their gills. They evolved in the Devonian Period. They are found in Australia, South America and Africa, and live on mudbanks. The 'lung', which is nothing but a modified swim bladder, helps them survive when their home pools dry up or they get stranded on riverbanks. They burrow into mud and breathe air with their lung.

▶ Lungfish have actually evolved from 4-footed land animals

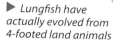

Antarctica

In spite of extreme weather conditions, wherein the area faces temperatures on the minus scale almost throughout the year, it does show a lot of biodiversity. Apart from penguins, seals, whales, and sharks, smaller fish live here as well. However, no amphibian can survive this harsh cold climate.

Antarctic toothfish is a species which inhabits the seas close to the continent. How does it survive the cold? The fish can produce anti-freeze proteins in its tissues and blood.

Another interesting species found in the Southern Ocean is the mackerel icefish. It too carries the anti-freeze protein as seen in most Antarctic fish. The icefish are white-blooded, meaning that they lack haemoglobin, the oxygen-carrying red pigment found in other fish. They have many adaptations in them, mainly in the cardiovascular system, which help compensate for the lack of haemoglobin.

To Swim or To Walk

Mudskippers are small, tropical fish that show amphibious characteristics. They live in the swamps and estuaries of eastern Africa, and the Indian and Pacific Oceans.

Mudskippers are about 30 centimetres in length. Their strong pectoral fins help their movement on land. They prey on shrimps and other very small animals. When in water, they breathe with the help of gills, just like all fish do. But on land, they use special gill chambers that fill up with water. This keeps the gills moist and functional for several hours on land. Also, mudskippers can take in oxygen through their skin.

▲ Antarctic toothfish live to almost 50 years of age

◀ The mudskipper goes on land to fight, hunt for food, and even to mate

Word Check

Alevin: It is the newly born salmon or trout fish.

Amnion: It is the membrane which encircles the embryo of a mammal, reptile, or bird.

Anadromous: It is a fish that migrates upstream in rivers in order to mate.

Antidote: It is a medicine that fights the effects of a poison.

Ballast: It is an organ that helps an animal (like the fish) maintain its depth in water without sinking or floating.

Calcareous: It is a shell made up of calcium carbonate.

Cartilaginous: It refers to animals that have a skeleton of cartilage, which is a soft connective tissue found in the body.

Catadromous: It means migrating down rivers to the sea to spawn.

Chordate: It refers to an animal that possesses vertebrae and belongs to the large phylum Chordata.

Dormant: It refers to species that are inactive.

Ectotherms: It refers to cold-blooded animals which depend on external heat sources to regulate their body temperature.

Electroreceptive organs: They are special organs in the skin of certain fish, which help them detect electric signals.

Endoskeleton: It is the internal skeleton.

Exoskeleton: It is the hard, external covering that is seen in invertebrate animals.

Gondwana: It is the continent that was formed in the southern hemisphere after the break-up of Pangaea. It later separated to form South America, Africa, Antarctica, Australia, Arabia, and the peninsula of India.

Hermaphrodite: It is a living organism that has both male and female reproduction organs.

Nervous system: It is a network of nerve cells and fibres that carry instructions to and from the different body parts to the brain.

Notochord: It refers to the cartilaginous skeletal rod that supports the body of an animal when it is at the embryonic (developing) stage.